CHARGE

TO THE GRAND JURY,

AT THE JULY TERM

OF THE

MUNICIPAL COURT, IN BOSTON,

1854.

By E. R. HOAR,

One of the Justices of the Court of Common Pleas of Massachusetts.

PUBLISHED BY REQUEST.

BOSTON:
LITTLE, BROWN, & COMPANY,
No. 112 Washington Street.
1854.

NOTE. — A report of the charge of Judge HOAR to the Grand Jury of Suffolk County appeared in the newspapers on the day following its delivery, and has been extensively circulated. The part of it which discusses "the relation of the military power to the civil authority of the Commonwealth" was written before it was delivered. The rest was oral, and more liable to verbal inaccuracies of the speaker or the reporter. Some of these have been corrected in this publication, but without departing, in any instance, from the substance of what was said.

BOSTON:
PRESS OF PRENTISS AND SAWYER,
No. 19 Water Street.

CHARGE.

AT the opening of the July term of the Municipal Court in Boston, on Monday, July 3, 1854, a new Grand Jury for the County of Suffolk was empanelled and sworn, and the Charge required by law was given by Judge HOAR.

He commenced by instructing the Grand Jury, at some length, upon the formal duties of their office, and upon the nature and obligations of the oath which they had taken.

He then proceeded to charge them particularly upon the laws prohibiting lotteries, referring especially to attempted evasions of those laws, under the name of Gift Enterprises, and Gift Concerts. He instructed the Grand Jury that such enterprises were infractions of the principles of the law, and that persons engaged in promoting those enterprises, or in selling or advertising tickets in them, were liable to indictment.

He then spoke of the fraudulent issue of the stock of corporations, and stated the rules of criminal law applicable to such a transaction. On this subject he held that if two or more officers of any corporation had fraudulently issued stock unauthorized by law, they were indictable for conspiracy; and if one officer alone had made such over-issue, and by that means had obtained money or other valuable things, he would be liable to be indicted under the statute for obtaining goods under false pretences. He then proceeded substantially as follows: —

Another subject on which I think it important that the law should be distinctly stated to you is, the subject of riots. It is matter of public notoriety, gentlemen, that riotous proceedings have taken place within the County of Suffolk, within this City, and recently. It is probable from the action of the inferior tribunals, that cases of this description may be brought before you, and it may be your duty to investigate that subject. I will, therefore, gentlemen, in the first place, state to you the legal definition of "Riot," and then state some of the rules applicable to persons engaged in riotous demonstrations.

"When three persons or more shall assemble themselves together with the intent mutually to assist each other against any who shall oppose them, in the execution of some enterprise of a private nature, with force or violence, against the peace, or to the manifest terror of the people, whether the act intended were of itself lawful or unlawful, — it is an *unlawful assembly:* and if they execute their enterprise to any extent, — it is a *riot.*"

You will notice, gentlemen, that to constitute a riot, there must be three persons, at least, or more assembled; they must be acting in concert, with intent mutually to assist each other against all who may oppose them. It must be in the exercise of a private purpose, to distinguish it from war or rebellion against the government. Now, gentlemen, there is no doubt, if three or more persons should assemble together with force and violence, and in a manner calculated to produce a breach of the peace, or to excite the terror of the people, with the intent to rescue a prisoner lawfully in custody, and should in the execution of that purpose proceed to batter down the door of a building in which that prisoner is held, that this would come within the legal definition of a riot. And, gentlemen, when an unlawful or riotous assembly exists, a responsibility may attach to all persons composing it, for the commission of an act beyond the intention of the persons who are thus unlawfully assembled — that is, beyond the particular intention of each individual — for the rule of law on that subject is this: —

"That if persons go together, united in an unlawful design, to commit a felony or breach of the peace, and in the course of effecting that purpose, any one does an act in pursuance of the common purpose, they are all answerable for it. But if one does an act, not in pursuance of the common design, the others would not be answerable."

In regard to the recent transactions which you are called upon to investigate, I am not aware that there is anything peculiar which will take them, in the investigation, out of the ordinary rules of law applicable to similar cases. It is not for me to assume facts, except so far as they may be matters of general notoriety, and you must investigate them for yourselves — that is your province, and not the province of the Court.

But it may be made to appear to you, that within a few weeks the door of this Court House was forcibly broken open, in the night time, by a large number of persons, and that in the course of the transaction in which they were engaged, a man lost his life; and that the purpose of those engaged in that assembly was to rescue from the custody of the Marshal of the United States, a person placed in his custody, under a precept issued by an officer of the United States. If the person whom he held were lawfully in his custody, an attempt by force and violence to rescue him, by three or more persons, carried wholly or partially into execution, would undoubtedly make them rioters; and if, in the course of their riotous acts, any person was by one of them, acting in pursuance of their unlawful design, killed, each of the persons who were thus engaged would be legally responsible for the death of that man, although it might not have been in their individual contemplation to take his life. If the common purpose were to rescue the prisoner by force, and by attacking those who had him in charge, and breaking down all opposition they might offer, and that led to the destruction of the life of one of the persons who had him in charge, or who was lawfully aiding the officers who had him in charge, that would render all responsible who were engaged in the common purpose.

Gentlemen, the question might be suggested whether this were a lawful prisoner. I suppose there is no question that he was held by the Marshal of the United States, under a precept from a Commissioner of the United States, and executing the authority which a statute of the United States had conferred upon him; and in relation to the question whether that statute were one creating a constitutional and legal obligation, I cannot, in the first place, so far as the facts have come to my knowledge, see that it can be material. For, gentlemen, if the statute had been unconstitutional, and if the prisoner were held merely under color of law, and not under a law that had any validity and was binding upon all citizens, the practical result might be the same. Men may do some things by force and violence; they may interfere to prevent a murder, for example. If at the time of the attempt to rescue the prisoner in the Court House, the men having him in custody were about to kill him, all citizens would have a right to attempt to rescue him in the quickest and most effective manner, however tumultuous. They would have the right to break in and prevent the commission of an irreparable injury, where the protection of the laws could not be made immediately available. In like manner, gentlemen, if a pirate should appear in our waters, and attempt to carry off a man or woman, the rushing together of citizens, with any degree of violence, to prevent such a deed, would be lawful; the exigency would justify the action. The law allows force to be used wherever, and to the extent that there is necessity for it, to prevent the commission of crime.

But, gentlemen, in the case which we are considering, I suppose no person would pretend that there was any intention to take the life of the man there detained; that there was any intention to do him bodily harm, or to do anything with him, except to detain him in the place where he was then held, until there should be an opportunity to resort to the ordinary civil tribunals. He was held there by an officer under the United States Government. Take the common cases of an arrest under a criminal charge, or for debt. An officer might be acting illegally, or under a precept which would not justify his action; yet, unless there were good reasons to apprehend that great and irreparable injury would be inflicted upon the person so held before he could be liberated by legal process, that would not authorize an assemblage of persons riotously to rescue him. They must resort to the ordinary tribunals, to the protection the law affords, to peaceable remedies, because tumult and violence might lead to greater evils than the one they were seeking to prevent.

Gentlemen, beyond this, it is my duty to say to you that the law under which that prisoner was detained, is a law binding upon the citizens of this Commonwealth. It has been enacted by the National Legislature, approved by the President of the United States, and held to be a constitutional enactment by that tribunal whose duty it is to determine the validity of all laws under which the inhabitants of this Commonwealth are placed; and whatever opinions we may individually entertain as to the correctness of that decision, no citizen of the Commonwealth has a legal right to disregard the decision of the Supreme Court. It is binding upon all. It is the duty of every inferior tribunal to regard what they have decided henceforth as law, and it is the duty of all those concerned in the administration of justice, in any and every department, so to regard it. Gentlemen, any other rule, any other conclusion, could lead to nothing but anarchy.

Undoubtedly, gentlemen, the decisions of the judicial tribunals of our country are subject to revision. We find the decisions of the Supreme Court of the present day overruling its decisions of twenty years ago. We find the Supreme Court of the United States overruling decisions which were made when that Court was differently constituted, holding that those decisions were erroneous and illegal, and it is competent for them to do so. And, gentlemen, the ultimate result upon any question of this nature, the ultimate decision of it, will be the result of the general conviction of the community. It will be the result of the mass of private opinion, at least of professional opinion in the community.

It may be that at some time hereafter, the act of Congress known as the Fugitive Slave Law will be held not to be constitutional. In the meantime, however, what is the duty of those of us who have to do with it in the administration of public justice? I might here, gentlemen, if it were proper for me to do so, and I were delivering an opinion in which that question arose, give you my private view upon this matter. I might say to you that the reasoning on which the law has been held to be constitutional, so far as our Supreme Court is concerned, as I understand the decision, is placed on the ground of authority, and not of right. I might say that the authorities upon which that decision rests have failed to satisfy my understanding. I might say, gentlemen, that in my view, regarding it in the best light I have upon the matter, that statute seems to me to evince a more deliberate and settled disregard of all the principles of constitutional liberty than any other enactment which has ever come under my notice. You, gentlemen, might each of you entertain similar private opinions upon this subject. But of what avail is it, and what right have you or I to act upon these opinions? It could never have been the intention of the framers of our Government, it is not consistent with the rules and principles of our Government, that a rule of law should be held one way in New York, another in Philadelphia, and another in Boston; that it should be dependent upon the individual opinion of a Judge or a Juror called upon to administer it. The only safe rule of our duty is, that when the tribunal, provided by the Constitution and laws, has decided upon the constitutionality of an enactment, all citizens are in practice bound to regard it as a question settled. With their political duties, with their feelings, we have nothing here to do. Within these walls nothing of party passion, of private interest or feeling, should come.

It has been said sometimes, and in some places, that there are laws which it is the duty of citizens to disobey or resist. I have no doubt, gentlemen, and I suppose none of you have any doubt, that a law may be enacted by a Republican Government, as well as an order passed by a despot, which may be in itself wicked; and if a statute is passed which any citizen, examining his duty by the best light God has given him, and acting conscientiously and uprightly, believes to be wicked, and which, acting under the law of God, he thinks he ought to disobey, unquestionably he ought to disobey that statute, because he ought to "obey God rather than man." I suppose that any man who would seriously deny that there is anything higher than human law, must ultimately deny even the existence of a Most High.

But, gentlemen, it is not a question of private conscience which determines our duties in the premises. A man whose private conscience leads him to disobey a law recognized by the community, must take the consequences of that disobedience. It is a matter solely between him and his Maker. He should take good care that he is not mistaken, that his private opinion does not result from passion or prejudice; but if he believes it to be his duty to disobey, he must be prepared to abide by the result, and the laws, as they are enacted and settled by the constituted authorities to be constitutional and valid, must be enforced, although it may be to his grievous harm. It will not do for the public authorities to recognize his private opinion as a justification of his acts. Gentlemen, in my last civil term in the county of Worcester, a case came before me in which a man, I believe sincerely, (probably he was partially deranged,) thought his religious duty required him to refuse to support his wife and children. He made that statement, whether it was through delusion, mistake, ignorance, or whatever other cause. I believe he rested it upon some passage of Scripture with regard to what a person might do with unbelievers, placing his family in that class, but the Court overruled his scruples. Although he might have a right, as between his Maker and himself, to act upon his conviction, it would not do to admit his private opinion and judgment, as to his right or duty towards his family, to weigh in the Courts of Justice with those called upon to administer the laws.

A case in which, from private conscience, a man can be bound openly to resist the law, by assailing others, it is more difficult to imagine. When such a case does arise, it partakes of the nature of a revolution; and all the considerations which apply to the right of revolution, and the expediency of attempting a revolution, apply to cases of that nature.

Gentlemen, recent occurrences in this city have made it my duty to instruct you upon another subject, of the highest importance to the peace and security of the community, and intimately connected with the principle which lie at the very foundation of our frame of government. I refer, as you already anticipate, to the relation of the military power to the civil authority of the Commonwealth. But a few weeks have gone by since the citizens of Boston saw in their midst a large body of soldiers assembled, the volunteer militia of Massachusetts, engaged, as it has been asserted, in preserving the peace of the city, and maintaining the supremacy of the laws — an honorable and responsible duty, whenever it is lawfully assumed, and faithfully discharged.

From what necessity or cause these soldiers were assembled; under what authority they acted; whether their employment and their conduct were in conformity with the Constitution and laws of the Commonwealth — and to whom the responsibility of their acts attaches — are questions which have been publicly discussed, and which it is not improbable that you may be obliged to investigate. The law applicable to them I shall endeavor as briefly and plainly as possible to state to you. And, gentlemen, while the chief reason for so doing is on account of the bearing it may have upon your practical duties, the occasion seems to me opportune, so far as it may aid in diffusing just sentiments and a distinct understanding upon a subject, concerning which precision of ideas is so important, and upon which so many confused notions seem to prevail.

With the holiday soldier — the bright array, the martial

music, and waving plumes, which most of us regard with complacency, and which afford such delight to the juvenile spectators, we are all familiar; with the soldier as the terrible instrument of the law, the last resort of the civil government for the absolute enforcement of its authority, we are happily unfamiliar. The cases in which it has been necessary to resort to an armed force to sustain the civil government of this Commonwealth have been of rare occurrence; and when such occasions have arisen, the moderation, prudence, and sound discretion of those who were entrusted with civil authority, and the firmness, forbearance, and exemplary deportment of the soldiers, have been such as to lead to no discussion as to the legality of their conduct.

It is extremely desirable, for the sake of the militia themselves, that the extent and limitations of their powers should be justly defined, and familiarly known. They wish to understand their duty and to do it. They are neither strangers nor aliens. Their interests are identical with ours. They are some of our acquaintances, friends, and neighbors, who have undertaken a particular public service. Interested in its more exciting and cheerful aspect, they are also willing to contemplate its more serious features. They are liable to be placed in trying situations, and upon a sudden emergency to be required to do acts of the most painful nature. The importance of an accurate apprehension of legal rights and duties, upon such a subject, can hardly be overrated. A duty more serious, a responsibility more fearful, can hardly devolve upon man, than that which belongs to the citizen soldier when lawfully summoned to aid the civil power in upholding or executing the laws. He should enter upon it in a serious and thoughtful spirit, regarding it only as a sad and terrible necessity.

Consider, gentlemen, for a moment, the sacredness with which human life is invested by the law, the solemnity which the lawful destruction of it everywhere assumes. The life of the vilest wretch among us, who has outraged all the laws of God and man, cannot be taken in the administration of public justice, and as the penalty of his crimes, but upon proceedings where every provision that the wit of man can devise is made against the possibility of haste, or error, or oppression. He must be indicted by a Grand Jury; the Supreme Judicial Tribunal of the State must be assembled; he must be found guilty by a jury, substantially of his own selection from a large number of the most discreet and respectable of his fellow citizens; able counsel are secured for him; he is to be notified beforehand of the names of the witnesses against him; and when his guilt has been fully established, no man has power to harm him, until the Supreme Executive shall have determined that there are no grounds for the interposition of its merciful prerogative, and have commanded the sentence of the law to be enforced.

In self-defence, in obeying the instinct of self-preservation, a man must retreat as far as he can, before he may lawfully resort to a deadly weapon, and slay his adversary.

But when a military force is employed to suppress a riot, a hundred lives may be sacrificed in a moment — without preparation, it may be almost without warning — the innocent with the guilty. The soldier who fires upon a mob may doom to instant destruction not only the lawless and depraved, but men of generous impulses and honest purposes — the *mistaken* — the *misled* — the *unwary* — those whom accident or curiosity have brought to the spot; perhaps his friend, his neighbor, his relative.

The public service which he is thus called upon to discharge is a subject for no boasting beforehand, or exultation afterward. No man of right principles or feelings could regard it lightly. He should go to it as he would go to attend an execution, and return thanking God for all that he had been rightfully permitted to leave undone.

It is sometimes said that our Government rests, at last, upon military force. It rests upon no such thing. It finds its chief strength in the respect of an intelligent and virtuous people for the laws which they themselves have made; and its ultimate reliance is upon the power of the people to execute their own will. The military force which a free people allow to exist among them, it regards but as a convenient instrument.

To understand clearly the points involved in this inquiry, it will be well to recur a little to first principles.

The object of a Constitution of Government is, in the preamble to the Constitution of Massachusetts, declared to be "*That every man may, at all times, find his security in the laws.*"

To this end two things were of the first necessity: 1, The maintenance and enforcement of such wholesome laws as should be enacted; and 2, The protection of the liberty of the citizen from the encroachments and abuse of authority of those to whom power should be intrusted. With a view to the first, the Constitution provides for the organization and government of militia; and, in reference to the latter, the Declaration of Rights contains this article: —

"The people have a right to keep and bear arms for the common defence; and as, in time of peace, armies are dangerous to liberty, they ought not to be maintained without the consent of the Legislature; and *the military power shall always be held in an exact subordination to the civil authority, and be governed by it.*" [Declaration of Rights, Art. xvii.

By the Constitution, the Governor is made the Commander-in-chief of the militia, and entrusted with full power to discipline, instruct, and govern them; and to employ them against the public enemies. He is also authorized to govern them by law martial, when in actual service, in time of war or invasion, and also in time of rebellion, *declared by the Legislature to exist;* with all the powers incident to his office, to be exercised agreeably to the Constitution and laws of the land.

His powers in respect to calling out the militia in case of war, insurrection, or invasion, made or threatened, are determined by law, (Rev. Stat., ch. 12, §129 and seq.) and are only to be exercised by the Governor in person, or in case of emergency by the commanding officer of a division.

With the nature of these powers and duties we have no immediate concern.

I come, then, to the question, What are the provisions of law for the suppression of riots and unlawful assemblies, and for executing the laws of the Commonwealth, when forcibly resisted?

These are of a two-fold nature: first, the modes which the common law authorizes, in the absence of positive enactment, and secondly, the powers expressly conferred by the statutes — each being, of course, limited and controlled by the principles of the Constitution.

I have already given you the definition of a riot or unlawful assembly — and by the common law any citizen may lawfully endeavor to suppress an existing riot, by resisting those who are engaged in it, and preventing others from joining them.

A sheriff, constable, or other peace officer, may do the same, and may command all other persons present to assist them.

He may also arrest any of the rioters whom he finds committing any breach of the peace, and take them before a justice. Any Justice of the Peace who shall find persons riotously assembled, may arrest them; and by a verbal command may authorize others to arrest them; and the persons so commanded may pursue and arrest the offenders in the absence of the justice, as well as in his presence.

The general principles of the law — that if any person is lawfully employed and is assaulted, he may use such force as is necessary in self-defence,— and that a person charged with the execution of a legal duty may repel, by force, any unlawful and forcible resistance to its performance,— apply in these cases.

The power of the Mayor and Aldermen of cities, and of the Selectmen of towns, to secure an adequate civil force by the appointment of police officers, is unlimited. (Stat. 1851, chap. 162.)

The statute of this Commonwealth which provides for calling out the militia to aid in the suppression of riots or tumults, and in executing the laws, is the statute of 1840, chapter 92, sections 27 and 29; and in all essential particulars it is an exact transcript of the 134th section of the 12th chapter of the Revised Statutes; with this exception, that it adds for the first time ***Mayors of Cities*** to the list of those by whom an armed force may be called out.

These sections are as follows: —

Section 27. "Whenever there shall be, in any county, any tumult, riot, mob, or any body of men acting together, by force, with intent to commit any felony, or to offer violence to persons or property, or by force and violence to break and resist the laws of this Commonwealth, or any such tumult, riot, or mob shall be threatened, and the fact be made to appear to the commander-in-chief, or the mayor of any city, or to any court of record sitting in said county, or if no such court be sitting therein, then to any justice of any such court, or if no such justice be within the county, then to the sheriff thereof, the commander-in-chief may issue his order, or such mayor, court, justice, or sheriff may issue his precept, directed to any commanding officer of any division, brigade, regiment, battalion, or corps, to order his command, or any part thereof, describing the kind and number of troops, to appear at a time and place within specified, to aid the civil authority in suppressing such violence and supporting the laws, which precept, if issued by a court, shall be in substance as follows: —

————————ss.

COMMONWEALTH OF MASSACHUSETTS.

[L. S.]

To { Insert the officer's title. } { A. B. commanding. } { Insert his command. }

Whereas, it has been made to appear to our justices of our————, now holden at————, within and for the County of————, that [here insert one or more of the causes abovementioned] in our County of————, and that military force is necessary to aid the civil authority in suppressing the same; now, therefore, we command you that you cause [here state the number and kind of troops required] armed, equipped, and with ammunition, as the law directs, and with proper officers, either attached to the troops or detailed by you, to parade at ———, on ———, then and there to obey such orders as may be given them, according to law. Hereof fail not at your peril, and have you there this writ with your doings returned thereon.

Witness, &c. * * * And if the same be issued by any mayor, justice, or sheriff, it should be under his hand and seal, and otherwise varied to suit the circumstances of the case."

Section 29. "Such troops shall appear at the time and place appointed, armed, &c. And shall obey and execute such orders as they may then and there receive, according to law."

The noticeable points of this Statute are, that it allows a military force to be called out not only when there is a riot, mob, &c., but whenever one is *threatened;* that it fixes the persons by whom the existence of the riot, &c., or the fact that one is threatened, shall be ascertained and determined; provides that the reason of calling out the military shall be stated in the order or precept; and then leaves the mode in which the troops shall be employed "to the civil authority in suppressing violence, and supporting the laws," to be fixed by the rules of the common law, or by other Statutes.

If summoned according to the provisions of this Statute, when they appear at the place named in the order or precept, they are lawfully assembled; — the fact that a sufficient necessity existed for their assembling is, so far as they are concerned, conclusively settled; and the question then arises, What may they lawfully do? To whose orders are they subjected? And how are such orders to be given?

In the first place, they have all the rights at common law, or under the general laws of the Commonwealth, which other citizens possess. "It is clear," in the language of an eminent Judge, "that the military do not lose the rights, and are not exempt from the duties of subjects, by entering into that condition."

They may occupy the place at which they were directed to appear, so long as by the orders which they may have received from the Governor, judge of a Court, sheriff, or mayor, or as they may there receive from any lawful authority, they are required to remain. They may march through the streets as on other occasions, not interfering with the reasonable use of the same by other persons; they may act in defence of their own persons and lives, if attacked or assaulted, using such force as is necessary and proper to repel the assailants.

They are not disqualified to act as the assistants of any civil officer who has the right to call on the citizens to aid him in the service of any process, civil or criminal, or in the execution of his duty under the laws; and although their being engaged in military service would be a sufficient excuse for not obeying any call upon them as individual citizens, by a person not authorized to direct the movements of the collective force, yet if they should obey the call, their acts would be in no degree unlawful, so far as those persons might be concerned against whom their acts were directed. If, without objection from their commanding officer, and without interfering with their obedience to any lawful orders given them, any of them should act as individuals to prevent a breach of the peace, or to stay a rioter, or arrest a felon, the right to do so would be as unquestionable as if they wore a different dress. For every injury done to them, or indignity offered, the offending person is, and ought to be, civilly and criminally responsible, as for a like offence to any other citizen; and with this aggravation of the wrong, that the very position which the soldier occupies, and the nature of his duties, may render it difficult for him to detect the offender, and take from him the power to make any resistance to the crime.

I come, then, gentlemen, to the consideration of the farther powers for suppressing tumults and enforcing the laws, which are contained in the 129th chapter of the Revised Statutes.

The first section provides that if persons to the number of twelve or more, being armed, or to the number of thirty, whether armed or not, shall be unlawfully, tumultuously, or riotously assembled in any city or town, the mayor and each of the aldermen of such city, and each of the selectmen of such town, and every justice of the peace therein, and the sheriff and his deputies, shall go among or near the persons so assembled, and require them to disperse; and if they do not disperse, then shall command the assistance of all persons present in arresting the offenders. The *second* and *third sections* provide for the punishment of officers neglecting or refusing to act, and of other persons who refuse or neglect to assist.

The fourth section authorizes any two of the officers before named, on the refusal or neglect of the unlawful assembly to disperse, to require the aid of a sufficient number of persons, in arms or otherwise, and to "proceed, *in such manner as in their judgment shall seem expedient,* forthwith to disperse" the assembly, and arrest the persons composing it.

The fifth section is as follows: —

"Whenever an armed force shall be called out, in the manner provided by the twelfth chapter, for the purpose of suppressing any tumult or riot, or to disperse any body of men acting together by force, and with intent to commit any felony, or to offer violence to persons or property, or with intent, by force and violence, to resist or oppose the execution of the laws of this Commonwealth, such armed force, when they shall arrive at the place of such unlawful, riotous, or tumultuous assembly, shall obey such orders for suppressing the riot or tumult, and for dispersing and arresting all the persons who are committing any of the said offences, as they may have received from the Governor, or from any Judge of a Court of Record, or the Sheriff of the county, and also such further orders as they shall there receive from any two of the magistrates or officers mentioned in the first section."

The sixth section, which is by a subsequent statute (1839, chap. 54, §1,) extended to all cases under the two preceding sections, provides that if by reason of the efforts made by any two of the said officers or magistrates, or by their direction, to suppress the unlawful assembly, &c., any person, though but a spectator, should be killed, the said magistrates and officers, and all persons acting under them, should be held guiltless; and, that if the officers or their assistants, or persons acting by their order, should be killed or wounded, all the rioters, and all persons who had refused to assist the magistrates or officers, should be held answerable.

It is apparent from this statute that it applies only to cases where a riot, tumult, unlawful assembly, or body of men collected with intent to do the unlawful acts referred to, actually *exists.* It authorizes no forcible acts, by way of precaution. And, gentlemen, none are authorized by law. The power to call out a military force, and hold them in readiness for the emergency when it shall arise, is given by the statute of 1840, to which I have previously referred. But the power extends no farther. And, as a practical rule, which will be decisive of some questions that may come before you, I shall instruct you that

There is no law in this Commonwealth by which any district, or part of a city or town, can be put into the possession of a military force in time of peace, with power to obstruct the ordinary and reasonable use of the public ways, and to prevent peaceable citizens from transacting their lawful business — merely on account of an *anticipated* riot.

The fact that a riot has previously taken place, unless it be continuous and existing, will not alter the rule of law. And if it shall be made to appear to you that a military force has been so employed within the County of Suffolk, and any man has been assaulted or injured thereby, or forcibly prevented from enjoying his ordinary rights as a citizen, without other justification under the law, every soldier who may have committed any such act of violence, and every officer, military or civil, who shall have ordered, requested, caused, or procured it to be done, is, (subject only to the qualification which I shall presently state,) to be held responsible therefor.

But it is asked whether, in a case where no man doubts that a riot or unlawful assembly is impending, the civil and military commanders are obliged to wait until irreparable mischief is done, till a prisoner is rescued, a building destroyed, or blood spilled, before they can fully interpose. A sufficient answer may perhaps be found in the statement, that they may employ all the ordinary and peaceable means of enforcing the civil authority, and may have in readiness for instant employment, any amount of military force which the exigency shall demand. Further than this the law does not go, and the magistrate or officer cannot. It may seem to many worthy and prudent men that more power should be granted; but it has not been thought necessary or expedient by the framers of our Constitution and laws. The principle of American institutions is not restraint — nor intimidation — but responsibility for acts done. In relation to freedom of speech, for example, and of the press, we do not, as in some countries it is done, establish a censorship, and determine beforehand what shall be spoken or published, but we leave men free to say or print what they please, and hold them accountable for any abuse of the liberty.

In the next place, gentlemen, the statute confers *no discretionary power* upon any military officer, under the commander-in-chief, nor can any be lawfully conferred upon him, except as to the details of executing a specific service, upon which he is lawfully ordered. And this is in strict conformity with the requirements of the Constitution, that "the military power shall always be held in exact subordination to the civil authority, and be governed by it." It is for the civil magistrates only to determine whether an unlawful assembly exists, and whether military power is needed to suppress it. If any civil magistrate should direct the commander of a military force, lawfully called out to aid in suppressing an anticipated riot, to take possession of a city or district, dispose his force therein as he should think expedient, and then, whenever in his judgment a riot should commence, or an unlawful assembly be gathered, to fire upon or disperse it — leaving the whole question of the occasion and the necessity to the discretion of the commander — such an order would be of no legal validity, and the military officer could not justify any act done under it, which would not have been legally justifiable if no such order had been given.

The details of military service must of course be left to the officer commanding the troops — but the service required must be designated by the civil authority. Thus, when a riot exists, the civil magistrates competent to act, may say to the officer, clear this street — dislodge the occupants of this building — disperse this assembly — arrest these rioters — protect these buildings — and the officer receiving the order may employ his force to execute it in such a manner as he may think best. He may send one file of men or ten; he may charge with bayonets or sabres; he may fire blank cartridges or bullets; he may, unless the order is countermanded, decide how many times he shall charge or fire, and when the assembly is sufficiently dispersed. But a general direction to preserve the peace of a city, and sustain the laws, can give to a military force no new protection or power.

On the other hand, if the orders given proceed from a competent civil authority,— although, in my judgment, the law clearly contemplates that the resources of the civil power should usually be applied so far as they reasonably can be, before resort is had to the military, yet a discretion is given to the civil magistrates to determine when military force is needed — and even if they have judged erroneously, the soldier who obeys those orders is protected — and the correctness of the decision cannot be questioned to his prejudice.

The statute further provides, that the discretion in the use of an armed force which it confers shall be exercised by two of the officers named in the first section jointly. It cannot be assumed by one alone. And further, the action of the two must be direct and positive. It is not sufficient that one shall be merely consulted by the other, and approve, or not object. Both must act. Both must assume the responsibility. It must be the order of both. Not that both must speak or write, but if one speaks for the two, it must be with a direct authority to speak in the name of the other.

The law plainly requires that both should be *present*. Not, of course, that they should be between the soldiers and the mob; not that they should ride with the military commander, or charge with his troops — but *present*, in a reasonable sense of that phrase applicable to the nature of the case; *present*, as a commander is present on the field of battle; *present*, so that they can have personal cognizance of the fact that military force is necessary; that they may direct its application, and be enabled to decide upon new exigencies as they arise, and to determine when the terrible necessity is ended.

There is, in my judgment, a strong and clear implication from the language of the 12th and 129th chapters of the Revised Statutes, although not so distinctly expressed as would be desirable, that the Governor, Judge of a Court of Record in any county, or Sheriff, may not only call out the militia, but in case of an existing riot, may give specific orders in regard to its suppression. This view is confirmed by the statutes of 1839, chap. 54, sect. 1, of which a part of the provisions could hardly have any intelligible effect, if it were not so. It is the general duty of the Governor to cause the laws to be executed, and it is a common thing to invest the Judge of a Court of Record with powers which it requires two inferior magistrates to exercise. It also seems to me that the actual presence of these higher officers of the State could not be contemplated or required. They must act upon evidence and information; and the Legislature must have supposed that the nature of their ordinary duties, and their relation to the Commonwealth, would ensure a competent knowledge of their legal power, and caution in its exercise.

The question has, I believe, no immediate practical bearing, but a statement of it seemed necessary to a complete view of the subject.

In Suffolk County, it could hardly arise, except in the case of the Governor or a Judge; as there is probably never a time when some Judge of a Court of Record is not found within this city, and the Sheriff would not therefore be called upon to act alone.

Another question of much practical importance is, how far the private soldier or the inferior officer is answerable for an act of violence done in obedience to the command of his superior, that command being given without lawful authority. If a captain order his company, who have been lawfully called out to aid the civil authority, to fire upon a crowd, or to drive back any persons who are passing along or across a street, or to clear a building, or the like, and the captain has no order from the commander of the force which would authorize him to give such a direction, or the commander himself has no legal authority from the civil magistrates, would the private soldier who should in good faith obey the order be protected? Unquestionably the person with whom the illegal order originated would be responsible to the fullest extent; and in respect to the subordinate, I shall instruct you substantially in the language of a recent decision of the Supreme Court of the United States.

Upon authority, and upon principle, independent of the weight of judicial decision, it can never be maintained that a soldier or military officer can justify himself for doing an unlawful act, by producing the order of his superior. The order may palliate, but it cannot justify. If the power exercised by the superior were within the limits of a discretion confided to him by law, the inferior would be justified by the order, even if the commander had abused his power. But I have already said that the law does not confide to him a discretionary power, except as to the mode of executing the lawful commands of the civil authorities. But there are cases when the soldier may be called upon to act in a sudden emergency, without the possibility of learning with absolute certainty the origin of the orders given him. If, in such a case, the subordinate act in *good faith* and with *due diligence,* acting upon such information as he had a right to rely upon, and upon all the information reasonably in his power to obtain, and which, if reliable, would render his act legal, the order of his superior will exonerate him from any *criminal* responsibility, although the information should afterward be discovered to be false or erroneous.

A point which may incidentally arise, respects the occasion upon which the troops were called out on the second of June last. It may be found that they were called out in aid of the civil authority, to preserve the peace of the city, which was endangered by a threatened resistance to the execution of a process of the United States. A few words upon this subject are all that are necessary.

We are all of us not only citizens of Massachusetts, but citizens of the United States. Our relation to the Government of the United States is a relation as individuals, except where the Constitution and laws of the Union have otherwise specially provided. The State militia cannot, as an organized force, be legally called into the service of the United States, except by a requisition of the President of the United States upon the Governor, and according to the Constitution and laws.

Our State officers have nothing to do, in their official capacity, with executing the laws of the United States. United States officers, if resisted in the discharge of their duty, may call upon citizens of the State to aid them in executing process, and it would be the duty and right of each citizen to obey the call, unless he were lawfully excused. A lawful excuse would be that the person whose aid was required was engaged in a public duty under the government of the State. Congress may confer upon officers of the United States powers to prescribe duties which are analogous to those of certain classes of State officers; but this can apply only to the discharge of their official duties under the laws of the United States, and can give them no authority to interfere with the execution of State laws, or to control or exercise any authority over any State organization, or to assume the specific functions of any State officer.

But, on the other hand, all acts done by an officer of the United States in the discharge of his duty are to be regarded as lawfully done under the laws of a State. And if, in resisting the execution of the laws of the United States, any breach of the peace should occur, or any other violation of State laws, it is the duty of the State officers to repress or punish it, as they would if it were happening to the injury or disturbance of any other citizens lawfully employed.

Thus, to apply these principles, the United States Marshal of a district has no official relation, as such, to a Massachusetts Justice of the Peace, or to the Mayor of a city, or Sheriff of a county. He cannot call out the militia of a State, nor give them any legal order when mustered, either alone or in concurrence with any State officer. Although Congress has conferred upon him the authority of a Sheriff, this obviously can only mean the same functions in executing the laws of the United States that a Sheriff has in relation to the laws of a State. He cannot serve a writ from a State Court, nor undertake to execute a State law. But these principles are too clear and well settled to require further illustration.

And now, gentlemen, it remains for you to apply the rules of law which I have given you.

If our citizen soldiers, lawfully mustered in the public service, have been assaulted or injured, see to it that the aggressor, if he can be discovered, shall not go unpunished.

If it shall be made to appear to you that any assault has been committed, or violence done, or forcible obstruction of lawful business occasioned, by any part of the military force, "diligently enquire and true presentment make" concerning it. Ascertain under what order or by what authority it was done. Trace it to its source. Consider what is its justification. Extend the full protection of the law to everything which a liberal construction of the law can justify or excuse. But if you find the law has been violated, and that there has been an invasion of private rights, or an infringement of public liberty, do your duty as you have sworn to do it; and "leave no man unpresented, for love, fear, favor, affection, or hope of reward."

It may be said that there was a great public exigency, an imminent danger; that riot and bloodshed were prevented; that there has been no considerable destruction of property, no serious personal injury inflicted; no sacrifice of life — and that it would be harsh and unwise to subject to criminal responsibility those who have acted with general good intention. Gentlemen, this is a very superficial view of the matter. All right-minded men are opposed to lawless violence. The whole community cry out against it. But when law is disregarded by its own guardians and supporters, it is "wounded in the house of its friends," and all sentiments of reverence for law in the public mind are weakened.

The old Latin maxim tells us, oppose beginnings — "*Obsta principiis.*" Occasions where the gravest consequences have not followed, and the strongest passions are not excited, are the best to establish principles and define duties.

And if the facts which shall be laid before you require it, I have no doubt, gentlemen, that you will be ready to show to the people of the State, that laws are not made for those only who crowd the gallery or fill the dock; that whenever the strong arm of power has been raised without justification, and any citizen has suffered in his person or property, the whole community feels the wound; and that the justice, which is no respecter of persons, will allow no military or civil title to give immunity to the transgressor.

www.ingramcontent.com/pod-product-compliance
Lightning Source LLC
LaVergne TN
LVHW020633110826
845149LV00004B/1167

9781418191405